BEARS

by JoAnn Early Macken

Reading consultant: Susan Nations, M.Ed., author/literacy coach/consultant

WEEKLY WR READER®
EARLY LEARNING LIBRARY

Please visit our web site at: **www.earlyliteracy.cc**
For a free color catalog describing Weekly Reader® Early Learning Library's
list of high-quality books, call 1-877-445-5824 (USA) or 1-800-387-3178 (Canada).
Weekly Reader® Early Learning Library's fax: (414) 336-0164.

Library of Congress Cataloging-in-Publication Data

Macken, JoAnn Early, 1953-
    Bears / by JoAnn Early Macken.
       p. cm. — (Animals I see at the zoo)
    Summary: A simple introduction to bears and some of their characteristics.
    Includes bibliographical references and index.
    ISBN 0-8368-3266-3 (lib. bdg.)
    ISBN 0-8368-3279-5 (softcover)
    1. Bears—Juvenile literature. 2. Zoo animals—Juvenile literature. [1. Bears.
2. Zoo animals.] I. Title.
QL737.C27M23   2002
599.78—dc21
                            2002016893

This edition first published in 2002 by
Weekly Reader® Early Learning Library
330 West Olive Street, Suite 100
Milwaukee, WI 53212 USA

Art direction: Tammy Gruenewald
Production: Susan Ashley
Photo research: Diane Laska-Swanke
Graphic design: Katherine A. Goedheer

Photo credits: Cover © Lynne Ledbetter/Visuals Unlimited; title, pp. 13, 17, 21 © James P. Rowan;
p. 5 © Diane Laska-Swanke; pp. 7, 15 © Joe McDonald/Visuals Unlimited; p. 9 © Greg W. Lasley/KAC
Productions; p. 11 © Fritz Pölking/Visuals Unlimited; p. 19 © Gerard Fuehrer/Visuals Unlimited

Printed in the United States of America

1 2 3 4 5 6 7 8 9 06 05 04 03 02

Note to Educators and Parents

Reading is such an exciting adventure for young children! They are beginning to integrate their oral language skills with written language. To encourage children along the path to early literacy, books must be colorful, engaging, and interesting; they should invite the young reader to explore both the print and the pictures.

Animals I See at the Zoo is a new series designed to help children read about twelve fascinating animals. In each book, young readers will learn interesting facts about the featured animal.

Each book is specially designed to support the young reader in the reading process. The familiar topics are appealing to young children and invite them to read — and re-read — again and again. The full-color photographs and enhanced text further support the student during the reading process.

In addition to serving as wonderful picture books in schools, libraries, homes, and other places where children learn to love reading, these books are specifically intended to be read within an instructional guided reading group. This small group setting allows beginning readers to work with a fluent adult model as they make meaning from the text. After children develop fluency with the text and content, the book can be read independently. Children and adults alike will find these books supportive, engaging, and fun!

— Susan Nations, M.Ed., author, literacy coach, and consultant in literacy development

I like to go to the zoo. I see bears at the zoo.

There are many
kinds of bears.
They live in
many places.
Black bears
live in forests.

Polar bears live
where it is cold.
Their thick fur helps
keep them warm.

Their fur blends
in with the snow.
The animals they
hunt cannot see
them.

Polar bears are good swimmers. They use their front paws to paddle.

Bears can stand
on their hind legs.
They sniff and look
around for food.

All bears have sharp **claws**. They can use them to dig for food.

claws

They can use
them to climb
trees. Bears
are good at
climbing.

I like to see
bears at the
zoo. Do you?

Glossary

blends — mixes together so that the separate parts cannot be seen

claws — sharp, hooked nails on an animal's foot

climb — to move up using the hands and feet

For More Information

Books

Macken, JoAnn Early. *Polar Animals. Animal Worlds* (series). Milwaukee: Gareth Stevens, 2002.

Sayre, April Pulley. *Splish! Splash! Animal Baths.* Brookfield, CT: The Millbrook Press, 2000.

Shahan, Sherry. *Feeding Time at the Zoo.* New York: Random House, 2000.

Web Sites

NATIONALGEOGRAPHIC.COM

www.nationalgeographic.com/kids/creature_feature/ 0010/brownbears.html

www.nationalgeographic.com/kids/creature_feature/ 0011/pandas.html

www.nationalgeographic.com/kids/creature_feature/ 0004/polar.html

For fun facts, video, audio, maps, and postcards to send to your family and friends

Index

About the Author

JoAnn Early Macken is the author of a rhyming picture book, *Cats on Judy*, and *Animal Worlds*, a series of nonfiction picture books about animals and their habitats. Her poems have been published or accepted by *Ladybug*, *Spider*, *Highlights for Children*, and an anthology, *Stories from Where We Live: The Great Lakes*. A winner of the Barbara Juster Esbensen 2000 Poetry Teaching Award, she teaches poetry writing. She lives in Wisconsin with her husband and their two sons.